Introduction

When the B&O Railroad completed the Metropolitan Branch line in 1873, new worlds opened. The farms of southern Montgomery County now had ready access to the markets of the City of Washington, DC. And it became possible for people to live in the country and commute to work in the city. New communities ("railroad suburbs") sprung up along the rail line - one of the first of which was Takoma Park, followed by Forest Glen, Kensington, Garrett Park, Washington Grove, and others.

In November 1883, Washington businessman and entrepreneur Benjamin Franklin Gilbert purchased 100 acres of the "Grammer Farm" from the heirs of Washington banker Gottlieb Grammer. Though called a "farm" there was likely little cultivation - ownership of large rural tracts was something of a status symbol among the Washington wealthy. These 100 acres, a mere six miles from downtown, straddled the Maryland and District of Columbia line around the current Takoma Station of the Washington Metro. Gilbert took the name "Tacoma" at the suggestion of his friend Ida Summy, changed the "c" to a "k" and added "Park." A small shed train station called Brightwood (the closest Washington community) was renamed Takoma Park. He subdivided the land, creating streets, blocks, and lots. A community was born.

Gilbert immediately began selling lots. The first were sold the same day he purchased the land. By 1884 the first house was built and small stores, including a post office, appeared around the train station. A hotel, livery, and other amenities soon followed. Many of Gilbert's purchasers were government officials from the Patent Office, the Agriculture Department, the General Printing Office, the Post Office, and other agencies. Some of the houses started as summer residences while others were occupied year around. This was country living with chickens, fruit orchards, wells, and water from nearby springs. Fifteen trains a day took commuters to Washington and back.

This pamphlet was published in 1886 by Gilbert as he began to promote his new community as a "high, healthful, convenient and pleasant place of residence." He stressed the elevation, no mosquitos, the lack of malaria, the pure air, and the improvements he made, while showcasing the early houses. He notes the affordability of owning a home in Takoma Park as well as the value of investing in Washington area real estate. Gilbert continued to expand his community - buying and subdividing lands to the east and north. In 1890 the Town of Takoma Park, Maryland was incorporated, with Gilbert elected as the first mayor. The rest, as they say, is history.

This pamphlet and many other aspects of Takoma Park's history reside in our archival collections. We are pleased to be a partner in sharing it with the Takoma Park community.

– Historic Takoma, Inc.
2024

A GOOD INVESTMENT

— FOR —

HOMES OR PROFIT:

THE VILLA LOTS OF

TAKOMA PARK,

A SUBURB OF

WASHINGTON CITY.

A High, Healthful, Convenient and Pleasant Place of Residence.

Altitude 350 Feet above the Level of Washington City.

NO MALARIA.

NO MOSQUITOES.

PURE AIR.

DELIGHTFUL SHADE.

A MOST ABUNDANT SUPPLY OF PURE WATER.

B. F. GILBERT,

REAL ESTATE (TAKOMA PARK,)

Office, 3 and 5 Pacific Building.

WASHINGTON, D. C.

1886.

THIS PAMPHLET has been prepared for the benefit of those who desire information relating to TAKOMA PARK, suburb of Washington City.

An attempt has herein been made to bring into prominent notice only those features that are apparent to every one making investigation, viz., the favorable conditions of nature that make TAKOMA PARK a most desirable place of residence, and the improvements that have already been made there.

Any further information will be furnished with pleasure at the office of

                B. F. GILBERT,
          REAL ESTATE (TAKOMA PARK,)
                  Rooms 3 and 5 Pacific Building.

WASHINGTON, D. C.,
    June, 1886.

A. G. GEDNEY, LITH.,
    POST BUILDING, WASHINGTON.

Takoma Park.

I.

An Outgrowth of Washington's Prosperity.

Washington City is progressing rapidly and putting on the best habiliments of modern civilization. It is rapidly taking rank amongst the great cities of America as a center of other interests than those of an entirely political character. The most refined natures find in it a habitation of genial surroundings. Science has made its home here. Literature and the Fine Arts are meeting with most happy encouragement. The people of the whole country feel a kindly interest in the welfare and prosperity of Washington City.

It is, indeed, the people who have adorned Washington with the most magnificent public buildings. They

---

Takoma Park, 350 feet above the level of Washington.

have erected enduring monuments to heroes, statesmen, and warriors; they have beautified its numerous parks and reservations, adorning them with imposing statuary, flowing fountains, and choice flowers; they have made it the beauty-spot of America.

The contrast between the old and new Washington is visible on every hand, so that the stranger and sojourner is filled with wonder and admiration. Both stranger and citizen behold with pride the noiseless reaching-out of its broad streets and avenues, and, as they mount the surrounding hilltops, the rising—almost like magic—of mansions and villas.

What Washington will be in the very near future is not a difficult question to answer. It has no rival—no opposition from any quarter. On the contrary, the whole Nation desires its prosperity; and since the people seem to have willed it, what is to prevent Washington from becoming the finest city in every respect on the American continent?

II.

The Suburban Residence.

One of the evidences of the thrift and permanent growth of a city is the tendency which is manifested among all classes to seek suburban homes. Many of the prominent citizens of Washington have country homes near the city, where they seek rural quiet and retirement after the business of the day is over. A drive in any direction about the city for three or four miles,

Pure air and pure water at Takoma Park.

and in some cases even further, will show evidences of this in the substantial houses standing back from the road amidst the trees and lawns. Many of these country homes, surrounded by cultivated farms, are occupied by men of means. In every direction around the city, in Maryland and Virginia, are small villages whose residents, to a large extent, are people whose business is in Washington. The subdivision of suburban property into building plats has been made to some extent, especially along the line of railroads, and flourishing settlements have sprung up. While naturally there are more people living in the country during the summer than in the winter, still a large proportion retain their country homes during the entire year. There are thousands of reasons why men desire to live somewhat away from the centre of a great city. No doubt a great many are drawn to the semi-country home for the sake of being where trees and grass and birds abound, while the little garden-spot affords a pleasant and healthful exercise. Perhaps it was some such sentiment as this that induced Laurence Sterne to say that there ought to be at the gate of every great city a guard whose duty it would be to challenge every stranger desiring to enter. If he could not show good cause for entering, the guard should turn him back into the green fields where Nature and the God of Nature could the more easily care for him.

The man of moderate means finds it possible to become the owner of his own home by going to the suburbs. The man of business finds rest; the invalid, health; children grow strong, and the aged find quiet.

Trees, flowers, and a garden-spot at Takoma Park.

RESIDENCE OF L. DUDLEY.

It would be impossible to name the thousand-and-one benefits and pleasures that arise from a residence in a healthful suburb, especially during the heated months of summer.

In the following pages will be found a brief description of one of the most flourishing and desirable places for country homes within easy reach of persons doing business in Washington.

III.

SITUATION AND NATURAL ADVANTAGES.

TAKOMA PARK is a natural outgrowth of the upward, forward movement of Washington City. It is a branch on the main stem of the prosperity of the Capital.

It is situated a little over five miles north of the City,

No mosquitoes at Takoma Park.

RESIDENCE OF DR. E. B. BLISS.

upon the Metropolitan Branch of the Baltimore and Ohio Railroad. A little more than two years ago the original tract was subdivided into liberal building sites. It lies on both sides of the railroad, and the District line also runs through it, so that a portion lies in Maryland (Montgomery Co.) and the remainder in the District of Columbia. The former name of the station, Brightwood, has been changed to Takoma. It may not be out of place here to call attention to the fact that Takoma is an Indian word and signifies "lifted up" or "near Heaven." The Indians applied this name to a lofty peak in Washington Territory.

The name is not inappropriately applied to TAKOMA PARK, for it lies 350 feet above the level of Washington City. It is, therefore, "lifted up;" and when we take

Absolutely, no malaria at Takoma Park.

into consideration the fact that the elevation above the surrounding country gives to TAKOMA PARK a most complete and natural drainage, thereby doing away with the conditions that engender and foster disorders of a malarial nature and the long train of diseases that are likely to follow, it is not an exaggerated expression to say that the place is an approach to Heaven.

Nature has certainly done much to make TAKOMA PARK a most healthful place of residence. She has supplied it most bountifully with

PURE WATER.

The water of TAKOMA PARK is of the very finest quality. It makes its appearance from springs that are crystal-like in their clearness, and goes flowing down the valleys in sparkling rivulets. In consequence of the impure state of the Washington City supply of water at certain seasons of the year, a number of families have been using the water from one of these springs, having it brought to them in barrels or demijohns. The spring is free to all.

No analysis of this TAKOMA PARK SPRING WATER has yet been made, and therefore it is not claimed that it has positive medical properties, yet it is a fact which can be well attested that many invalids have been greatly benefited by its use. The water is simply *pure*. It is a well-established fact that the efficacy of "mineral water" does not depend on the quantity of its mineral constituents. A medical writer says on this point,

---

Fifteen trains a day between Washington and Takoma Park.

"Chronic malarial troubles are wonderfully relieved in many cases by springs whose mineral constituents thoroughly evade discovery, and certain intractable dyspeptic disorders are cured by them in a manner which I am unable to explain."

It seems, therefore, that it is not necessary that water should hold a drug-store in solution in order to be of great value as a curative agent. All who attempt to live in health ought to have good air and good water; these two elements being pure, give life;—being impure, they take it away.

The water from the TAKOMA PARK Spring is now on draught at the Drug Store of Harry Standiford, southwest corner of 9th and F streets.

The purest water is also reached in wells at a distance from the surface of 12 to 25 feet. Many wells have already been dug, and in doing so it has been observed that after penetrating the surface some feet, a strata of fine terra-cotta clay is met. Immediately under this is a layer of white gravel, which becomes finer as the well is deepened until it results in a white sand. Here a vein of the purest of water is obtained in inexhaustible quantity. The strata of clay renders it impossible for any surface water to penetrate to the fountain of the well. These wells have been sunk in all parts of TAKOMA PARK with the most perfect satisfaction.

The face of the ground is of a rolling character—enough so at least to give a most pleasant diversity to the landscape, which is covered with a great variety of trees.

Low rate of railroad fare---quarterly tickets.

Residence of B. F. Gilbert.

Trees.

The pine, which is quite plentiful, exhales a most delightful odor, which seems to add to the purity of the air.

The tulip-poplar, oak, chestnut, maple, magnolia and the shrub-like holly and laurel also abound. While the growth of timber is not large, it is of a sufficient size to produce most ample and delightful shade.

IV.

Improvements that have been made at Takoma Park.

About two years have elapsed since, taking advantage of the natural conditions of this location, the first steps

Takoma Park—high, healthful and beautiful location.

were taken to bring it into subjection as a place of suburban residence. It was subdivided into spacious lots, with convenient streets and avenues between. The lots have a frontage of fifty feet and a depth of two to three hundred. The streets and avenues are forty to fifty feet in width, with a space on either side of twelve feet for parking and walks. Then the building regulations provide that each house shall stand back forty feet from the line of the side-walk—leaving, therefore, all told, a space of one hundred and twenty feet between the building lines. The streets have all been graded and the most important of them have been covered with a coating of gravel. The work is still being carried on from time to time, as the necessity of it appears. It has been done wholly at the individual expense of the proprietor.

It is only necessary to call attention to the illustrations in this pamphlet in order that the reader may have an idea of the quality of building improvements that have been going on at TAKOMA PARK. The pictures have all been prepared from photographs taken from the buildings as they now stand at TAKOMA PARK. Only a part of the number already finished and occupied by the owners is here presented.

There are now about one hundred and fifty residents at TAKOMA PARK. More are waiting for houses to be finished, when they will move in.

Those who are already there take evident pleasure in beautifying their immediate surroundings by preparing lawns, walks, flower-beds, setting out hedges and mak-

Malaria is unknown at Takoma Park.

ing gardens; thus adding comeliness and a completeness to the naturally beautiful landscape.

For the banker, the lawyer, the merchant and the clerk, no better, cheaper or more wholesome relief from the daily cares, toils and vexations of business can be found than that afforded by becoming a resident of TAKOMA PARK. The simple fact that he has a night's rest in the cool and quiet country, away from the heat and noise and the noxious airs of the busy city, is enough to add new life to a man, not taking into account the benefits and profits derived from the morning and evening hours of "fixing up" about the new home.

These pleasures and benefits are within the reach of all who choose to avail themselves of the opportunities now presented. At TAKOMA PARK one has the advantages of both the city and the country, for the many local trains which run to and from Washington at almost every hour in the day and night, and the low rates of fare, give all the benefits in the way of school, business, and pleasure, that are enjoyed by those who live in the city, the difference in the cost of living being in favor of those who live at TAKOMA PARK.

THE BALTIMORE & OHIO RAILROAD.

This is not only the oldest, but it is one of the most comprehensive and prosperous corporations of the time. Its extension to a terminous on the eastern seaboard,

Stop paying rent—own a home at Takoma Park.

at one of the finest harbors on the coast, marks a new era in the history of transportation.

This new combination will give Washington another independent through highway to New York and eastern connections; and not only does it indicate a reduced rate of fare, but the scenery through which it passes is of great beauty.

With the increased east and west traffic which this new connection will cause to flow over the line of the B. & O. Railroad by the way of Washington, will come the necessity of a double track over the Metropolitan Branch of this road. This project has already been taken into consideration by the Company, and has been entertained with so much favor that it is thought by those who ought to know that it will be carried into effect in the near future.

Under what is known as "Circular No. 7," the B. & O. Railroad Co. has organized a special department for the substantial encouragement of such places located on its line as TAKOMA PARK. This is done by seeing that all needed railroad facilities are provided, such as new and additional side-tracks, station-houses, freight depôts, and by making certain concessions in fares and freight rates.

The Company is now erecting a fine station-house at TAKOMA PARK. The architectural plans and specifications in the hands of the constructor show a passenger-house of sufficient size to supply the needs of a population of 5,000 to 8,000 people; and when we take into consideration the well-known conservative principles

---

Short ride by rail; pleasant drive by road.

RESIDENCE OF O. D. SUMMY.

upon which this railroad is operated, this one circumstance speaks volumes for TAKOMA PARK. With sagacious foresight the B. & O. has seen the future in the present.

The passenger-house has a beautiful exterior. It provides separate waiting-rooms, and offices for tickets, telegraph, baggage, &c., and a covered pavilion.

RAILROAD FACILITIES BETWEEN WASHINGTON AND TAKOMA PARK.

The Baltimore and Ohio Railroad Company is now running eight local trains one way and seven the other, over their Metropolitan branch, all of which stop at TAKOMA PARK. It gives assurance that these train facilities will be increased as rapidly as the growth of population will justify.

Fifteen trains a day between Washington and Takoma Park.

The B. & O. Railroad Co. has also made the following concessions to builders and residents at TAKOMA PARK:

The transportation over its road of household effects, and building material for dwellings, at one-half current freight rates, according to classification.

The transportation of workmen employed in making improvements, at one-half the regular rates, during the time employed.

Free care and transportation on passenger trains of marketing and other household supplies, not too bulky in character, to holders of commutation tickets.

Trains are now running between Washington and TAKOMA PARK, as follows:

METROPOLITAN BRANCH B. & O. R. R.

Trains Leave Washington—	*Trains Leave Takoma Park—*
6.45 A. M.	7.22 A. M.
*8.40 A. M.	*8.04 A. M.
10.05 A. M.	9.28 A. M.
12.30 P. M.	11.35 A. M.
4.40 P. M.	2.37 P. M.
*5.31 P. M.	3.28 P. M.
11.20 P. M.	*5.10 P. M.
	*7.55 P. M.

Trains marked * run daily.

THE DRIVES TO TAKOMA PARK.

TAKOMA PARK having its location but a short distance north of Soldiers' Home, all of the popular and

Commutation rates about 5 cts. per trip.

most fashionable drives which lead to the latter place are also available in reaching TAKOMA PARK. All of these, viz., Lincoln Avenue or Harewood Road, Seventh Street and Fourteenth Street roads, are the best made and the best kept highways that leave the city in any direction. Therefore, as every Washingtonian knows, there is no more popular drive than that to Soldiers' Home. When the proposed extension of Vermont Avenue is made, it will also lead directly to Soldiers' Home, and passing on through, will intersect the District line at TAKOMA PARK.

PROFITABLE INVESTMENTS.

The rapid growth of Washington City makes it one of the most attractive places for profitable investments in real estate in the country. During the ten or fifteen years just past, such investments have yielded large profits, and many fortunes have been made.

The future promises still greater inducements to the capitalist, for there can be no doubt but that the growth of Washington is of the most permanent character. Her citizens are moving in certain enterprises which, when accomplished, will add to the lasting glory of the Capital City. Among these may be mentioned the extension and improvement of certain streets and avenues northward, the erection of a magnificent free bridge across the Potomac, and the establishment of a permanent exposition. These measures are now before

Take a trip to Takoma Park and see a beautiful place.

Congress with most flattering prospects of favorable consideration in each case.

Takoma Park villa lots offer most favorable opportunities for profitable investments.

Prices and Terms.

Full information in relation to prices and terms will be furnished upon application at the office of B. F. Gilbert, rooms 3 and 5, Pacific Building. Prices range from $1\frac{1}{4}$ to 5 cents per foot. Terms to suit the purchaser. Lots contain 10,000 to 25,000 square feet each.

It will be found upon inquiry by those interested that a very moderate income will enable one to become the owner of his own home at Takoma Park. A stone quarry has been opened on the grounds, from which builders are allowed to take stone for foundations at the actual cost of quarrying and hauling. Sand for mortar is also accessible at the cost of hauling. In consequence of these and other favorable arrangements the expense of building at Takoma Park is very much reduced.

Many Department clerks are paying out sums as monthly rentals that would buy a home at Takoma Park if applied as purchase money.

A commodious store building is now being erected near the depôt at Takoma Park. When completed, a general stock adapted to the necessities of the community will be kept constantly on hand.

Low prices and easy terms for lots at Takoma Park.

RESIDENCE OF A. C. CORY.

A new tract has just been subdivided and added to TAKOMA PARK, in which lots are sold at a very low figure.

Persons desiring to see TAKOMA PARK can make arrangements at Mr. Gilbert's office for free passage and escort.

Persons at a distance desiring information in regard to investments for profit in and about Washington City, will receive prompt attention by addressing B. F. Gilbert, Pacific Building, Washington, D. C.

Historic Takoma, Inc.

Historic Takoma is an all-volunteer, non-profit organization established in 1979 to preserve, protect, and promote the history, culture, and built environment of Takoma Park, Maryland and the Takoma Park neighborhood of Washington, DC through education, advocacy, research, and archival collections.

Historic Takoma sponsors talks, events, walking tours, and other activities including the annual Takoma Park House and Garden Tour and maintains extensive archive and reference collections in its building at 7328 Carroll Avenue in Takoma Park, Maryland.

Support and learn more about the work of Historic Takoma at HistoricTakoma.org

www.ingramcontent.com/pod-product-compliance
Lightning Source LLC
LaVergne TN
LVHW010446070526
838199LV00066B/6218